Nobody Listens to Andrew

story by Elizabeth Guilfoile

pictures by Dora Leder

HOUGHTON MIFFLIN

Boston • Atlanta • Dallas • Geneva, Illinois • Palo Alto • Princeton

Andrew saw something upstairs.

He ran down very fast.

He said,

"Listen, Mother."

Mother said,

"Wait, Andrew.

I must pay Mrs. Cleaner.

She must catch the bus before

dark."

Andrew said,

"Listen, Daddy.

I saw something upstairs."

Daddy said,

"Wait, Andrew.

I must cut the grass before dark."

Andrew said,

"Listen, Ruthy.

I saw something upstairs.

It was in my bed."

Ruthy said,

"Wait, Andrew.

I must put on my roller skates.

I want to skate before dark."

Andrew said,

"Listen, Bobby.

I saw something upstairs.

It was in my bed on the sun

porch."

Bobby said,

"Don't bother me, Andrew.

I must find my bat and ball.

I want to play ball before dark."

Andrew said,

"Listen, Mr. Neighbor.

I saw something upstairs.

It was in my bed on the sun porch.

It was black."

Mr. Neighbor said,
"Never mind, Andrew.
I must take my dog for a walk
before dark."

Andrew said very loud,
"Listen, Mother,
Listen, Daddy,
Listen, Ruthy,
Listen, Bobby,
Listen, Mr. Neighbor,
Listen, Mrs. Cleaner,
THERE IS A BEAR UPSTAIRS
IN MY BED."

Mother stopped paying Mrs. Cleaner.

She said, "Call the police!"

Daddy stopped cutting the grass.

He said, "Call the fire department!"

Ruthy stopped skating. She said,
"Call the zoo!"

Bobby stopped playing ball.
He said, "Call the dog catcher!"

Mr. Neighbor stopped taking his
dog for a walk.

He called the police.

He called the fire department.

He called the dog catcher.

He called the zoo.

"Zoom!" came the police.

"Zing!" came the fire department.

"Whoosh!" came the dog catcher.
"Swish!" came the man from the
zoo.

They all ran upstairs.

"Look!" said Mother.

"It is on the sun porch."

"Look!" said Daddy.

"It is black."

"Look!" said Bobby.

"It is on Andrew's bed."

25

"Look!" said Ruthy.

"It is a bear.

Andrew said it was a bear.

But nobody listens to Andrew."

The dog catcher caught the bear
in his net.

The firefighter said,
"It climbed up the tree.
It climbed in the window."

The man from the zoo said,
"It is dry in the woods.
The bears are thirsty.
They are looking for water.
I will take this bear to the zoo."

Daddy said . . .

"Next time we will listen to Andrew."